For the Love of
GOLDEN
RETRIEVERS

For the Love of
GOLDEN
RETRIEVERS

Robert Hutchinson

BROWNTROUT PUBLISHERS
San Francisco

Golden Retriever Photography Credits

Cover		©1998 Sharon Eide & Elizabeth Flynn
p.2/3		©1998 Kent & Donna Dannen
5		©1998 Denver Bryan
6/7		©1998 Kent & Donna Dannen
8/9		©1998 Kent & Donna Dannen
10/11		©1998 Kent & Donna Dannen
12/13		©1998 Kent & Donna Dannen
14/15		©1998 Mark Raycroft
16		©1998 Mark Raycroft
17		©1998 Alan and Sandy Carey
18/19		©1998 Alan and Sandy Carey
20/21		©1998 Mark Raycroft
22/23		©1998 Alan and Sandy Carey
24		©1998 Sharon Eide & Elizabeth Flynn
25		©1998 Zandria Muench Beraldo
26/27		©1998 Mark Raycroft
28/29		©1998 Kent & Donna Dannen
30/31		©1998 Alan and Sandy Carey
32		©1998 Mark Raycroft
33		©1998 Mark Raycroft
34		©1998 Kent & Donna Dannen
35		©1998 Mark Raycroft
36/37		©1998 Kent & Donna Dannen
38/39		©1998 Kent & Donna Dannen
40/41		©1998 Mark Raycroft
42/43		©1998 Mark Raycroft
44/45		©1998 Zandria Muench Beraldo
46		©1998 Mark Raycroft
47		©1998 Jerry Shulman
48/49		©1998 Zandria Muench Beraldo
50		©1998 Mark Raycroft
51	(upper)	©1998 Mark Raycroft
51	(lower)	©1998 Zandria Muench Beraldo
52/53		©1998 Mark Raycroft
54/55		©1998 Mark Raycroft
56		©1998 Denver Bryan
57	(upper)	©1998 Kent & Donna Dannen
57	(lower)	©1998 Kent & Donna Dannen
58/59		©1998 Sharon Eide & Elizabeth Flynn
60		©1998 Mark Raycroft
61		©1998 Mark Raycroft
62		©1998 Jerry Shulman
63		©1998 Mark Raycroft
64/65		©1998 Alan and Sandy Carey
66		©1998 Mark Raycroft
67	(upper)	©1998 Kent & Donna Dannen
67	(lower)	©1998 Mark Raycroft
68/69		©1998 Mark Raycroft
70		©1998 Kent & Donna Dannen
71	(upper)	©1998 Jerry Shulman
71	(lower)	©1998 Kent & Donna Dannen
72/73		©1998 Mark Raycroft
74		©1998 Kent & Donna Dannen
75		©1998 Mark Raycroft
76/77		©1998 Alan and Sandy Carey
78		©1998 Mark Raycroft
79		©1998 Mark Raycroft
80		©1998 Kent & Donna Dannen
81		©1998 Kent & Donna Dannen
82/83		©1998 Sharon Eide & Elizabeth Flynn
84		©1998 Mark Raycroft
85	(upper)	©1998 Mark Raycroft
85	(lower)	©1998 Scott McKiernan/Zuma
86/87		©1998 Kent & Donna Dannen
88/89		©1998 Kent & Donna Dannen
90/91		©1998 Kent & Donna Dannen
92		©1998 Sharon Eide & Elizabeth Flynn
93	(upper)	©1998 Alan and Sandy Carey
93	(lower)	©1998 Mark Raycroft
94		©1998 Mark Raycroft
95	(upper)	©1998 Alan and Sandy Carey
95	(lower)	©1998 Mark Raycroft
96/97		©1998 Mark Raycroft
98		©1998 Mark Raycroft
99		©1998 Mark Raycroft
100/101		©1998 Alan and Sandy Carey
102		©1998 Mark Raycroft
103		©1998 Mark Raycroft
104/105		©1998 Mark Raycroft
106/107		©1998 Mark Raycroft
108/109		©1998 Mark Raycroft
110/111		©1998 Kent & Donna Dannen
112		©1998 Kent & Donna Dannen

Library of Congress Cataloging-in-Publication Data
Hutchinson, Robert, 1951—
    Golden Retrievers / Robert Hutchinson.
        p.   cm. — (For the love of—)
    ISBN 1-56313-901-4 (alk. paper)
    1. Golden Retriever.   I. Title.   II. Series:
Hutchinson, Robert, 1951–   For the love of—
[SF429.G63H87   1997]
636.752'—DC21   97-23666
                                                         CIP
                                                         r98

Printed and bound in Italy by Milanostampa

ISBN: 1-56313-900-6 (alk. paper)
10 9 8 7 6 5 4 3 2 1
Digit on the right indicates the number of this printing

Published by:
BrownTrout Publishers, Inc.
Post Office Box 280070
San Francisco,
California 94128-0070 U.S.A.

Toll Free: 800 777 7812
Website: browntrout.com

PURE GOLD

Everybody has thrilled to the slow-motion ballet of the Golden Retriever whirling high through the air to snag a hovering Frisbee. Everybody has admired the easy dignity of the Golden Retriever photographed beside its presidential or royal master. Everybody has marveled at the lustrous mantle of golden filaments adorning the Golden Retriever taking Best-in-Show at Crufts or Westminster.

But only a happy few have tasted the deepest joys of this breed. Only its owners have basked in the boundless adoration, loyalty, and lovingness of a Golden Retriever's gaze. Only its owners have delighted in their children's giddy play with the sweetest of playmates. Only its owners have felt the visceral surge of pride when a Golden Retriever dives with stylish abandon far over the water after its appointed quarry.

Who is this superb creature — in its native element whether air, earth, or water — itself a being of fire?

9

RETRIEVER, GOLDEN

The Golden Retriever is one of six Retrievers bred in the United States today. The other Retriever breeds are the Labrador Retriever, the Chesapeake Bay Retriever, the Flat-Coated Retriever, the Curly-Coated Retriever, and the Nova Scotia Duck Tolling Retriever.

Currently, two of the four most popular dog breeds in the United States are Retrievers. The Labrador Retriever ranks first (158,366 AKC registrations in 1997); the Golden Retriever comes in fourth (70,158). The Chesapeake Bay Retriever is modestly popular (5,204). The remaining three Retriever breeds are rare (fewer than 500 apiece). Although the six breeds differ in popularity, they have much in common.

The first feature that the six Retriever breeds in the United States have in common is that all were created to do the same job. Retrievers were originally bred in the nineteenth century to retrieve for hunters the dead or wounded birds that they had shot out of the air over land or water. Nowadays, many Retriever dogs are bred for show or companionship rather than the field. As a result, each Retriever breed has split into two sub-breeds: the field dog, judged for performance; and the show dog, judged for beauty. Even so, modern lines of Retriever dogs that have not been bred to the field retain their ancestral retrieving aptitudes in large — albeit diminishing — measure.

The second feature that the six Retriever breeds have in common is that they all share ancestors. A seminal ancestor to the foundation stock of each one of the Retriever breeds is the Lesser St. John's Newfoundland, an extinct Canadian maritime fishing dog. The Lesser St. John's went directly into the foundation of our modern Retrievers in the cases of the Chesapeake Bay Retriever (about 1810); the Nova Scotia Duck Tolling Retriever (1860); Flat-Coated Retriever (1870); and the Labrador Retriever (1880).

In addition, the Lesser St. John's entered every one of the Retriever breeds secondarily, through cross-breeds themselves derived from the Lesser St. John's. The Flat-Coated Retriever and its extinct predecessor, the Wavy-Coated Retriever, were both developed by cross-breeding the Lesser St. John's with Setter. The Flat- or Wavy-Coated Retriever, in turn, contributed importantly to the Golden Retriever (from 1870) and the Labrador Retriever (from 1890). The extinct Tweed Water Spaniel, a cross between the Lesser St. John's and the Tweed Water Dog, contributed importantly to the Curly-Coated Retriever (from 1830) and the Golden Retriever (from 1870).

As well as a considerable proportion of Lesser St. John's, the foundation stock of each of our modern Retriever breeds carried some mixture of traditional Spaniel and Setter. In addition to this grounding in traditional Setter, three of the Retriever breeds (Golden; Chesapeake Bay; and Nova Scotia) received infusions of Red Setter (the ancestor of the modern Irish Setter) to help stabilize desirable coat-colors.

The modern Retriever breeds have so much common blood, both from common precursory breeds and from early interbreeding amongst themselves, that in their formative years most of them were not even granted independent status by the national breed associations on either side of the Atlantic. Until this century, Retrievers were registered by the Kennel Club of England as *Flat-Coated, Curly-Coated, Liver-Coloured,* or *Norfolk* Retrievers. These subdivisions were not genuine breeds but simply phenotype descriptions. A single Retriever litter often contained representatives of several of these phenotypes. Such litter diversity resulted not only from the inherent difficulties in "fixing" breed traits but also from the deliberate practice of "infolding" the various strains that prefigured our modern Retriever breeds in order to promote vigor (*heterosis*).

Only in 1903 did the Kennel Club begin to register Labrador Retrievers as such. Not until 1913 were Golden Retrievers registered as a distinct Retriever breed in the country of their origin. In the United States, the American Kennel Club recognized the Chesapeake Bay Retriever as an independent breed in 1878, but registered the dogs corresponding to all our other modern Retriever breeds *indifferently as Retrievers* until the late 1920's. The Golden Retriever was not recognized by the AKC until 1932.

Given all the congruences and interminglings in their breeding histories, it is not surprising that the Retriever breeds show broad similarities in temperament and behavior. All the Retriever breeds typically show inexhaustible retrieving drive; joy in the sights and sounds of the hunt; delight in diving and swimming; lively intelligence in operating flexibly within complex learned routines *(sagacity)*; slow mental maturation; stable and cheerful disposition; unconditional love toward master; affability toward strangers; hardness against pain; and negligible attack instinct.

Different fortes in this shared repertoire distinguish one Retriever breed from another. Labs rule the field trials; Chessies dominate the open water; Curlies hunt upland fur as eagerly as they retrieve lowland feather; Flat Coats best combine show conformation and field skills in the same individual; Nova Scotias specialize in suckering ducks with a zany busker routine.

And the Goldens? They are well-rounded enough as Retrievers to win at anything: field trials; tracking; guiding. But with their fluid carriage, their sparkling intelligence, their solicitude to please, and their glamorous good looks, Golden Retrievers effortlessly surpass all their cousins in obedience competition and in the show ring.

The gilded beauty and graceful manners of the Golden Retriever did not just happen. They were patiently sublimed from the raw materials of many common breeds by a lord — a gentleman-breeder who for a quarter of a century devoted unlimited serious leisure, unstinting capital, and systematic habit to the pursuit of a singular aesthetic vision. No other Retriever breed owes its existence to a single man. It is fortunate indeed that he left a continuous record of his work, which allows us more than a century later to trace the quest for the Golden Retriever in gorgeous detail.

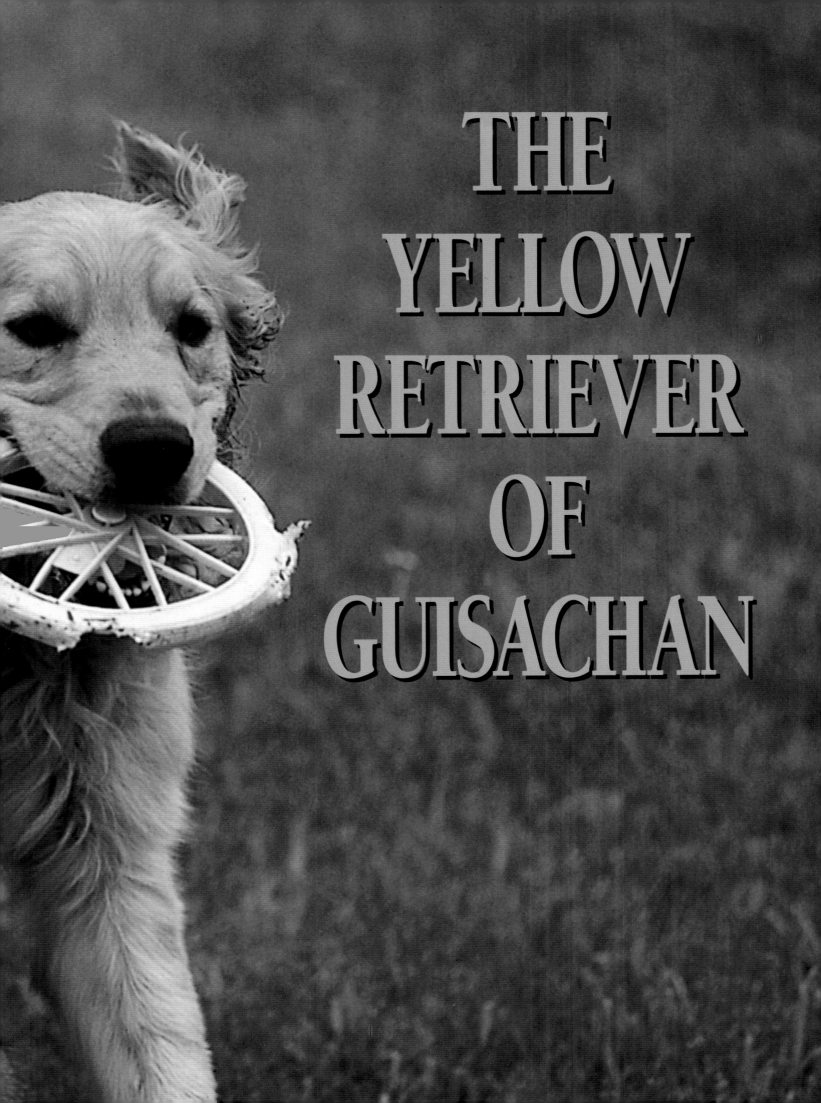

The Golden Retriever breed was developed in Scotland by an English peer. The first Lord Tweedmouth — as Sir Dudley Marjoribanks was styled — resided at Guisachan House. Tweedmouth is an English community at the mouth of the River Tweed, four miles south of the border with Scotland. Lord Tweedmouth's castle-like home, Guisachan, was nestled in a Highlands glen near the head of Beauly Firth, twelve miles west of Inverness.

In 1865, Lord Tweedmouth visited the south coast of England, bought a yellow Wavy-Coated Retriever in Brighton bred by the Earl of Chichester, and brought him back to Guisachan. The dog, named **Nous,** was the only yellow in a litter of black Wavy-Coated Retrievers. Nous was rather big and had a wavy coat. Lord Tweedmouth picked him to be the foundation stud of the yellow retriever breed that he envisioned.

Stabilization of yellow in the breed line was not the challenging part of Tweedmouth's program. Yellow is a recessive trait

in Retrievers. Dark pigmentation is entirely eliminated from a breed line as long as yellows are mated to yellows. Lord Tweedmouth saved that perfunctory step for the end. His real challenge was to sculpt a sound and beautiful dog fit to wear the golden mantle. From 1865 to 1889, Lord Tweedmouth meticulously recorded every step in his yellow retriever breeding program.

In 1867, Lord Tweedmouth was given a Tweed Water Spaniel by his cousin, Mr David Robertson, MP from Ladykirk on the Scottish side of the salmon-rich River Tweed, twelve miles upriver from Tweedmouth. The liver-coated Tweed Water Spaniel bitch was named **Belle.**

In 1868, Nous sired four yellow bitches out of Belle, one of which he named **Cowslip** (after the yellow flower). In 1873, Cowslip was outbred to another of Mr Robertson's liver-colored Tweed Water Spaniels to produce **Topsy.** In 1876, Cowslip was crossbred to a Red Setter to produce **Jack.** In 1877, Topsy was outbred to the black Flat- or Wavy-Coated Retriever **Sambo** to produce **Zoë.** Zoë was then inbred to Jack (her half-uncle) to produce yellow **Gill** and **Nous** II. In 1882, Gill was outbred to the black Flat- or Wavy-Coated Retriever **Tracer** to produce black **Queenie.** In 1889, Queenie was inbred to yellow Nous II (her uncle) to produce **Prim** and **Rose.** These two puppies are the last yellow-retriever entries in Lord Tweedmouth's breeding records. Although the Guisachan kennel-keepers continued to breed for yellow retrievers thereafter, the second Lord Tweedmouth kept no records.

Lest the second Lord Tweedmouth be unjustly suspected of indolence, it should be observed that he was obliged to attend to a very busy ministerial career, which included appointments in successive Liberal administrations as Keeper of the Privy Seal, First Lord of the Admiralty, and Lord President of the Council. As a matter of fact, it was the political influence of the second Lord Tweedmouth that enabled his young nephew — Winston Churchill — to launch his own ministerial career in 1906.

In 1894, a photograph was taken of a yellow retriever bitch named **Lady** belonging to the first Lord Tweedmouth's youngest son, the Honorable Archie Marjoribanks. Lady appears in the photograph to be of appropriate age to have been bred out of Prim or Rose. The connection remains, however, undocumented. It is documented, however, that Archie Marjoribanks sold two yellow retrievers out of a daughter of Lady to the first Viscount Harcourt.

These two dogs were presumably the foundation stock of Viscount Harcourt's breed line of yellow retrievers leading from Sulphur and Melody; through Dust and Chlores (registered in 1901); to Culham Brass (registered in 1903) and Culham Copper (registered in 1905) — the prepotent sires of the Culham Kennel who are the fountainhead of the whole Golden Retriever breed.

In 1908, Viscount Harcourt entered the first *Golden Flat-Coat* in a show. In 1912, *Golden Flat-Coats* scored their first wins in field trials. In 1913, the Golden Retriever Club was founded in England. Prior

to 1913, yellow retrievers from Guisachan-Culham lines were registered by the Kennel Club of England as color-qualified *Flat-Coats*. From 1913 until 1920, yellow retrievers of Guisachan-Culham descent were registered as *Golden or Yellow Retrievers;* since 1920, as *Golden Retrievers*.

There are two hiatuses in the record of the Guisachan-Culham lineage. The first hiatus occurs between the last yellow retrievers in Lord Tweedmouth's record book and Lady. The second hiatus occurs between Lady's grandchildren and the first yellow retrievers in the Culham Kennel records. Although the genealogical links over these hiatuses can only be conjectured, no reasonable doubt attaches to the proposition that Lord Tweedmouth laid

the foundation of Golden Retriever breed. The continuity of the Guisachan-Culham lineage is supported by the identical appearance of the Guisachan and Culham yellow retrievers in photographs as well as by the documented transactions between the successive breeders.

Given that Lord Tweedmouth's linebreeding program gave us the Golden Retriever, a careful description of his program's last recorded yellow retrievers (Prim and Rose) in terms of their breeding history is highly relevant to our modern breed. Two forms of measurement are conventionally used to describe consanguinity in an individual's pedigree: inbreeding coefficient and "blood".

The Coefficient of Inbreeding is an estimated measure of the percentage increase

in the residual homozygosity of a study animal that results from the duplication of ancestors in the pedigrees of both the sire and the dam. As calculated by Willis' formula (1968), Prim and Rose are inbred 13.3% on common ancestors Jack, Zoë, and Cowslip. To get an idea of the significance of this measurement, we can bracket our 13.3% with inbreeding coefficients from other contexts. On the lower side, the child of a first-cousin marriage between human beings is inbred 6.3%. On the higher side, a representative dog in the early German Shepherd Dog breeding program, separated from that breed's founder by the same number of generations as Prim and Rose are separated from Cowslip, was inbred 39.1% on three common ancestors.

The degree of inbreeding in the early Golden Retriever far exceeded the legal limits for human beings, as it must if selected traits were to become "fixed" in the breed line. Yet the degree of inbreeding in the early Golden Retriever was considerably less than in some other early breeds, reflecting Lord Tweedmouth's frequent recourse to crossbreeding to enlarge the menu of traits from which to select his perfect dog. (Unrecorded crossbreeding may have continued under the second Lord Tweedmouth, whose nephew suggested that "savage" Bloodhounds may have been crossed into the Guisachan yellow retriever line sometime in the 1890's. Certainly, evidence of such a cross is absent from the appearance and temperament of the Culham Golden Retrievers.)

The other method of measuring consanguinity in a pedigree is to reckon up the fraction of a study animal's "blood" (total genes) that it has inherited from a given ancestor by counting one-half for a parent, one-quarter for a grandparent, etc. For example, progeny out of a father-daughter mating is reckoned to carry three-quarters of the "blood" of the sire. This method, popularized by Francis Galton (1869), yields only a notional approximation of true inheritance. Although a dog inherits exactly half of its "blood" from each parent, it does not inherit exactly a quarter of its "blood" from each grandparent. Because meiosis is a random process, the fraction of an individual's total genes that is inherited from a given grandparent can vary anywhere from one-half to zero. Still, simple

additive "blood" fractions do hold on average. Because Jack was both their paternal grandfather and their great-grandfather, Prim and Rose each carried (1/4 + 1/8), or 37.5%, of the "blood" of Jack. Prim and Rose carried 37.5% of the "blood" of Zoë; 28.1% of the "blood" of Cowslip; and 14.1% of the "blood" of Nous.

This approach can be adapted in the reverse direction to estimate the fractional contributions of each of the crossbreeds to the "blood" of Prim and Rose. Go back along each branch in the pedigree, stopping whenever you reach a pure Wavy Coat, Tweed Water Spaniel, or Setter. Then reckon the "breed-blood" fractions of each purebreed's descendants forward to Prim. This is admittedly something of a fool's

game: Breeds are sociolinguistic constructs, not genetically transmissible traits. But, taking into full account the inherent fuzziness of the exercise, it is still a suggestive way to profile the new breed.

By "breed-blood" reckoning, Prim and Rose were each composed of 58% **Flat-** or **Wavy-Coated Retriever**; 23% **Tweed Water Spaniel**; and 19% **Setter.** Because the Flat- or Wavy-Coated Retriever and Tweed Water Spaniel breeds were themselves each the product of crossbreeding, the breed composition of Prim and Rose can be further reduced to second-order breeds, as we will show.

First we will briefly describe the breeds that were folded into the Guisachan line of yellow retrievers. The first-order component breeds were the Flat- or Wavy-Coated Retriever; the Tweed Water Spaniel; and the Red Setter. The second-order component breeds were the common Setter; the Lesser St. John's Newfoundland; the Tweed Water Dog; and the Springer Spaniel. We will then re-calculate the "breed blood" of the ultimate Guisachan yellow retrievers in terms of the second-order breeds. Finally, we will impressionistically compare our calculated results with the modern Golden Retriever.

The most important first-order component breed (accounting for 58% of the "breed-blood" of Prim) in the Guisachan line of yellow retrievers was the **Flat-** or

Wavy-Coated Retriever. Three sires (**Nous, Sambo,** and **Tracer**) in the pedigree of Prim and Rose were of that breed. Flat- or Wavy-Coated Retriever denotes a single breed insofar as Flat Coats and Wavy Coats both came about by crossing **Setter** and **Lesser St. John's Newfoundland**. Wavy-Coated Retrievers appeared in the first half of the nineteenth century as the result of unsystematic "best-to-best" breeding by diverse sportsmen. According to Stonehenge (J.H. Walsh) in *British Rural Sports* (1857), the Wavy-Coated Retriever dog was variously black, black-and-tan, brindled, or liver; at least twenty-four inches in height; and seventy to eighty pounds in weight. Stonehenge failed to remark that yellow Wavy Coats occurred, too.

Flat-Coated Retrievers appeared in the 1870's as the result of a systematic breeding program conducted

by the first president of the Kennel Club, S.E. Shirley. Shirley's linebred Flat Coats gradually displaced outbred Wavy Coats, but the change in the dog was nominal except for stabilization of coat-color. Flat Coats were preferentially bred to be of uniform black or liver color. Yellows popped up persistently in early Flat Coat litters. Before the recognition of the Golden or Yellow Retriever in 1913, true yellow Flat Coats could be registered with the Kennel Club but were generally considered less desirable. No colors but black and liver are accepted in modern Flat Coats. When the occasional yellow Flat Coat still pops up, it is culled. Yellows are rare today but not valuable.

Of the two second-order breeds going into the Flat- or Wavy-Coated Retriever, the Setter was a land dog and the Lesser St. John's was a sea dog. The traditional Setter was a bird dog developed over the course of six centuries. Its job was to locate quarry; creep up on it; crouch (*set*) near it; point to it with a paw; rise and flush it on the hunter's command; and retrieve it if appropriate. Its dimensions were the same as those of the Flat- or Wavy-Coated Retriever. Its variegated coat was fringed (*feathered*) on the ears, chest, legs, and tail.

The Lesser St. John's was developed as a water dog for the dory-fishermen who worked the cod-rich southern shore of the island of Newfoundland with hook-and-line or seine.

The dogs leapt into the frigid Labrador Current to fetch lines and fish to the boat or to maneuver net floats as bidden. The Lesser St. John's, according to Colonel Hawker in *On Shooting* (1820), had a short coat, usually black but sometimes light cream, and was about the same size as the Flat- or Wavy-Coated Retriever. Its oily double-coat was impermeable; its size small enough to work from a two-man boat. To navigate in heavy seas, the Lesser St. John's had a thick rudder-like tail. Some late nineteenth-century writers ascribed webbed toes to the Lesser as well as the Greater St. John's Newfoundland.

Traditionally, most authorities have inclined to the view that the Lesser St. John's was most likely developed from some English water dog

brought over by Devonshire fishermen, stationed in Newfoundland since the early sixteenth century. More recent research (laid out in this book's companion, *For the Love of Labrador Retrievers*) has been examining the alternative possibility that an old Portuguese breed called the Castro Laboreiro was seminal to the Lesser St. John's.

Nomenclatural confusion surrounds the extinct Lesser St. John's Newfoundland. First, the Lesser must be distinguished from the Greater St. John's Newfoundland, from which the modern Newfoundland breed is directly descended. The latter was an entirely distinct type, developed in Newfoundland as a giant draft and rescue dog. (Sir Edwin Landseer gave his name to the black and white variety of the Greater St. John's Newfoundland that he depicted as the hero of his 1856 sea-rescue painting, *Saved.*) Throughout the nineteenth century until 1885, the Lesser and Greater types were imported by the English, who generally lumped them together indiscriminately as Newfoundlands or as St. John's Dogs. To add to the confusion, when the Lesser St. John's Newfoundland was distinguished from the Greater, it was variously called the **Lesser St. John's Dog,** the **Lesser Newfoundland,** or the **Labrador** — the last even though no association existed between the dog and the mainland region of that name. Finally, this early *Labrador* is quite distinct from our modern *Labrador* breed, which dates only from the last decade of the nineteenth century.

Although distinct, the modern Labrador and the Lesser St. John's Newfoundland are closely related. Prior to the Quarantine Act of 1885, a number of aristocratic English kennels regularly imported Lesser St. John's Dogs to be bred in estate lines for gun-work. In their separate kennels, the successive Dukes of Buccleugh and the successive Earls of Malmesbury maintained Lesser St. John's lines "as pure as [they] could". The crossing of these two lines in 1882 yielded the direct ancestors of all modern Labrador Retrievers. The modern Labrador diverged from the Lesser St. John's Newfoundland during the course of extensive crossbreeding with the Flat-Coat Retriever after 1882.

After the Flat- or Wavy-Coated Retriever, the next biggest first-order breed component (accounting for 23% of the "breed-blood" of Prim) in the Guisachan line of yellow retrievers was the Tweed Water Spaniel. Two ancestors in the pedigree of Prim and Rose were Tweed Water Spaniels. According to Stonehenge, the Tweed Water Spaniel was a little smaller than the Retriever, with a curly liver-colored coat and a heavy muzzle. According to Richard Lawrence in *The Complete Farrier and British Sportsman* (1816), the Tweed Water Spaniel was derived by crossing the **Tweed Water Dog** and the **Springer Spaniel**.

Of the two second-order breeds going into the Tweed Water Spaniel, once again

one was a land dog and the other a sea dog. The Springer Spaniel, like the Setter, is an ancient sporting dog developed to flush *(spring)* birds. Its coat is also long and feathered, but the Springer Spaniel is considerably smaller than the Setter.

The other second-order component of the Tweed Water Spaniel — the extinct Tweed Water Dog — was a big, broad-shouldered, thick-necked animal with a short curly coat of variable color. It was developed to retrieve birds shot along the North Sea coast north of Tweedmouth and fallen into the breakers or onto the ruined limestone sea-cliffs. The Tweed Water Dog itself comes from a third-order cross between the **Water Dog** and, yet again, the **Lesser St. John's Newfoundland**. The origin and character of the Water Dog are obscure; Lawrence fancied some "Greenland Dog" extraction.

The smallest first-order breed component (accounting for 19% of the Prim's "breed blood") in the Guisachan line of yellow retrievers was the Red Setter. One sire in the pedigree of Prim and Rose was of that breed. The Red Setter is subsumed under the general description of the Setter given above, except that its feathered coat was selected to be silky and of a color ranging from chestnut to mahogany. Being the size of an ordinary Setter, the Red Setter of the nineteenth century was a smaller dog than its modern Irish Setter descendant.

On the simplifying assumption that each of the two crossbreeds in the Flat-Coat Retriever and in the Tweed Water Spaniel accounted for half of the resultant breed, the first-order "breed-blood" percentages given above for Prim and Rose can be reduced to these second-order components: 47% **Setter**; 35% **Lesser St. John's Newfoundland**; 12% **Springer Spaniel**; and 6% **Water Dog**.

Three considerations encourage us to extrapolate these percentages from the flowers of the Guisachan line to today's Golden Retriever. First, no crossbreeding is known to have been done to the Culham descendants of the Guisachan line. Second, today's Golden Retrievers look just like the late Guisachan dogs depicted in numerous photographs and paintings. Third, Prim's proportions of 59% land dog and 41% water dog accord well — in an impressionistic way — with the profile of the modern Golden Retriever.

All the outstanding performance traits of the Golden Retriever on land — tractability (*biddability*); sagacity; retrieving instinct; bird mania; drive;

agility — find their types in the Setter and the Springer Spaniel. The Golden Retriever possesses a parallel set of traits adapted to water sport. The traits that the Golden Retriever shows in the water — biddability; sagacity; retrieving instinct; drive; swimming strength; high pain threshold (*hardness*) — were salient traits of the Lesser St. John's Newfoundland (and also, presumably, of the Water Dog). In addition to all these water-adapted traits, the Tweed Water Dog showed bird mania and derring-do at the water's edge, as does the Golden Retriever.

Physically, as well as behaviorally, the Golden Retriever is prefigured by its various component breeds. The feathering of the Golden Retriever's coat is also shown by the Setter and

the Springer Spaniel. The rich copper of the darker end of the golden gamut of the Golden Retriever's coat-color resembles the lighter end of the color gamut of the original Red Setter. The color gamut of the early Golden Retrievers ran from the fox red of the Red Setter to the light cream of the double-recessive color-variant of Lesser St. John's. The waterproof double coat of the Golden Retriever is structured like that of the Lesser St. John's. In depth of brisket, shortness and strength of loin, straightness and bone of foreleg, and breadth of skull, the Golden Retriever is comparable to the Lesser St. John's. In overall length-to-height ratio, setting of forequarters and tail, and length of head, the Golden Retriever is comparable to the Setter.

Temperamentally, the pacific disposition of the Golden Retriever is mirrored in all of its component breeds, none of which was noted for aggressiveness. The slowness of mental maturation and the lifelong playfulness of the Golden Retriever are also consistent with its component breeds. Slowness of mental maturation is a function of the longer development time for superior intelligence. Lifelong playfulness is a manifestation of sagacity. These features endear Golden Retrievers to human beings, a species which displays even more pronounced neoteny.

We have examined in some depth the many ingredients that Lord Tweedmouth blended into the Golden Retriever. It remains to inquire as to Lord Tweedmouth's motivation in devoting a quarter of a century to the perfection of his four-legged Pygmalion.

Hunting has ever been the especial preserve of the aristocracy in Britain. In no other pastime could an English gentleman display to better advantage his wealth, his leisure, his command over man and nature, and his deadliness. The breeding of sporting animals was a necessary practical corollary to the hunt. It also reinforced the breeder's display of wealth, leisure, and command over nature. Breeding was, furthermore, an endeavor that heartily recommended itself to men whose privilege and assurance of innate superiority depended on their own pedigrees. In the class society that was England, nothing was more ostentatiously English than hunting and breeding.

In the 1850's, Victoria and Albert developed Balmoral, in the Scottish Highlands fifty miles southeast of Guisachan, as a crenellated mock-medieval castle. The royal couple, perceived by many of their subjects as German aliens, were deeply unpopular at the time. At Balmoral Castle, Victoria and Albert attended to the serious business of legitimizing themselves as British sovereigns by posing in well-publicized media events as tartan-clad lairds out of a Sir Walter Scott romance.

The hunt figured as a central motif in the lore of the Highland chieftain. Victoria and Albert's patronage of Sir Edwin Landseer — whose paintings of Albert's royal hunts in Scotland (most famously, his stag portrait, *Monarch of the Glen*) were even more widely reproduced than his paintings of Landseer Newfoundlands — helped de-Germanize Albert's public image. It also helped transform the Sassenach image of Scotland from that of a backward wasteland to that of a Romantic setting for the blood sports of the English aristocracy.

English aristocracy flocked to Scotland with a passion to shoot that the Monarchs of the Glen were far too few to gratify. Fowl-shooting offered much more bang than the buck. Far from being an idle hobby, Lord Tweedmouth's yellow retriever breeding program at Guisachan was a serious and timely affirmation of aristocratic taste and prerogative.

Until Lord Tweedmouth undertook in 1865 to develop a yellow retriever breed, retrievers had, like setters and pointers, been bred exclusively for field performance. Almost as much color variation was countenanced in the English sporting breeds as in its herding breeds. By 1865, however, a striking precedent for breeding for uniform color had been set on the Continent. In the mid-nineteenth century, the Leonberger dog was developed in Germany expressly to imitate a lion in appearance. The Leonberger's coat-color had attained a sufficiently stable leonine yellow by the end of the 1860's that Empress Elizabeth of Austria was pleased to add to her retinue this new courtier in the guise of the King of Animals. Royalty across Europe, including the Prince of Wales, enthusiastically followed suit.

In the 1860's, imperialist rivalry between the German and English ruling classes was already intense. In the high-prestige arena of dog breeding, the British had long enjoyed an unassailable sense of superiority. The recent German success in breeding a golden dog as a royal mascot posed a sharp challenge. Patriotic one-up-manship may well have played a part in the motivation of Lord Tweedmouth's breeding program. What a resounding proof of English good sense if he were to breed a golden *retriever* — fully as useful in the royal hunt as it would be beautiful in the royal court!